LET'S TALK ABOUT IT:
SEXUALITY

A SIX WEEK COURSE

MORAL REVOLUTION

KRIS VALLOTTON &
HAVILAH CUNNINGTON

Cover Design & Layout by Hans Bennewitz

Special Thanks to Soo Prince for your amazing efforts in this project!

TABLE OF CONTENTS

SMALL GROUP GUIDELINES

This Student Guide is written in such a way that it can be used for individual or group study alongside the Let's Talk About It: SEXUALITY, The Teacher's Guide, DVD series or as a resource to fill in while taking part in the live teaching sessions. This page is given to help you use it as a small group resource.

How to Start a Small Group
To start a group you will need a copy of the Let's Talk About It: SEXUALITY, The Teacher's Guide and the DVD series and then each group member will need a copy of this Guide.

No-one involved in the small group you set up needs to be a teacher or have had any previous experience with group work. You all just need to be willing and committed to meeting together, being open and vulnerable, taking it in turns to host and lead/facilitate each week.

Each talk is about 30 minutes long so we suggest each time you meet that you go no longer than 2 hours. This is our suggestion, but obviously tailor it to suit your group.

- 15 minutes for greeting, preparing refreshments and getting everyone settled
- 30 minutes for going through the Connection and Memory verse sections
- 30 minutes DVD watching
- 45 minutes for going through the Love It and Live It sections

It's a good idea for every group to share their expectations so we recommend you discuss these in your first session in order to lay a healthy foundation. The following are values you might want to consider, but feel free to modify any of them or add your own.

In being part of this group, we agree to the following:

Group Attendance
To give priority to attending and to call if I am absent or late.

Safe Environment
To create a safe place for people to share, be heard and be vulnerable.
I will not try to 'fix' anyone in the group or judge them.

Safe Relationships
To avoid gossip and keep good relationships by speaking directly to the person I am experiencing conflict with.

Spiritual Growth
To give group members permission to speak into my life and help sharpen me.
This will cause accelerated growth for me!

UNDERSTANDING YOUR STUDENT GUIDE

Here is a brief explanation of the features of this Student Guide.

 DVD: There is a DVD of each lesson for the group to watch together every week. Fill in the blanks in the lesson 'Learn It' section as you watch.

 CONNECTION: Open up each group meeting by sharing your experience of the journey you have been on since the previous week.

 MEMORY VERSE: For each lesson you will see there is a key verse to memorize. Have people look it up in different translations to get a fuller idea of the message behind the verse! Have fun testing each other. (The key word being FUN!)

 LEARN IT: This section is to use as you watch or listen to the lesson and fill in the blanks as you go. [Hint: there is an Answer Key at the back that you can refer to later if you are unsure of the missing word(s)].

 LOVE IT: Each lesson has further questions for you to use for group discussion. Don't feel under pressure to do every single one! The idea is to stimulate thought, create focus and hope and ultimately lead to a greater hunger and motivation for change.

 LIVE IT: Our heart's desire is that you connect deeply with the lesson material and are motivated to journey with God outside of the actual lesson teaching and group time. So here in this section we have come up with more reflective questions for each of you to complete in your own time with God. These, of course, can be brought to the group to share as part of the 'Connection' time if you would like, but there is no pressure or obligation to do so!

 BEYOND THE BOOK: This section contains more resources relevant to each lesson, to add the richness of your experience of each lesson material. Things like reading, video links, testimonies, articles, blogs etc. Enjoy!

01 | SEX & GOD

- How You Learned About Sex
- God Created Sex
- Character of God

🔌 CONNECTION

- If you are using this Student Guide as a small group and it's your first time meeting together as a group, spend time connecting.
- Before you jump into this study, we recommend that you review the Small Group Guidelines on page 2 of this Student Guide.
- What are you hoping to get out of this study?

_____

_____

_____

_____

MEMORY VERSE

"The Lord is slow to anger, abounding in love and forgiving sin and rebellion."
Numbers 14:18 (NIV)

LEARN IT

QUESTION: How and where did you learn about sex?

The environment you grew up in will have shaped your knowledge and perspective on sex. In understanding the filter you have—formed from your particular environment—you will hopefully gain more insight on why your view of sex may not match entirely with God's.

The Silent Environment
In this environment we learned sex is neither good nor bad; it is simply not talked about. Whether due to fear, ignorance or privacy, no time was given to teaching you the value of sex. It left you with a lack of information and the feeling that sex is not important. You are left to explore the topic on your own and you might conclude: "If the most important people in my life don't place value or importance on sex, why should I?"

We learn sex is not _____

The Saturated Environment
This environment is very vocal about sex. It is expressed in the form of jokes, movies, media and casual relationships. The crude and disrespectful way it is talked about communicates the opposite of the true significance and purpose of sex and cheapens the connection. You might conclude: "Sex is nothing more than a physical act and anything else experienced is over-thinking a simple encounter."

We learn sex is just a _____

The Conflicted Environment

This environment sends mixed messages about sex. It is communicated that sex has value within marriage and is full of shame outside of marriage. This results in confusion and potentially leaves you with an inability to manage your sexual desire outside of marriage. It's harmful because you end up following a rule of "don't" out of fear; without a personal connection to the "why" you don't. This means that in the heat of the moment your desire "trumps" the rule. We know enough to aim for purity, but don't always manage to maintain it. You might conclude: "I'm just going to try and do what's right, because it's right, and hopefully I won't blow it."

We learn sex is both _____ and _____

QUESTION: What does God think about sex?

God created sex. He's very passionate about it and has a lot to say about it. Sex is all throughout the bible.

"God made humans in his image reflecting God's very nature. You're here to bear fruit, reproduce lavish life on the Earth, live bountifully!"
Genesis 9:6–7 (VOICE)

God_____ sex

We can't overlook the significance of God creating man and woman as a reflection of the Trinity and the first command is to engage in the sexual embrace[1].

"He created humanity in His image, created them male and female. Then God blessed them and gave them this directive: "Be fruitful and multiply"."
Genesis 1:27–28 (VOICE)

The purpose of sex is to be _____ &

_____

Wendell Berry explains, "sexuality…is centered on marriage, which joins two living souls as closely as, in this world, they can be joined. This joining of two who know, love, and trust one another brings them in the same breath in the freedom of sexual consent and into the fullest earthly realization of the image of God. From their joining, other living souls come into being, and with them great responsibilities that are unending, fearful, and joyful."[2]

QUESTION: What is the true character and nature of God?

LIE #1—God Can Reject You

TRUTH: The nature of God is *unconditional* love. He is for you and wants you to succeed. He'd have to reject Himself to reject you.

"So, what do you think? With God on our side like this, how can we lose? If God didn't hesitate to put everything on the line for us, embracing our condition and exposing himself to the worst by sending his own Son, is there anything else he wouldn't gladly and freely do for us? And who would dare tangle with God by messing with one of God's chosen? Who would dare even to point a finger?"
Romans 8:31–33 (MSG)

God's love for me is _____

LIE #2 —When He is Hurt or Angry, God Can Ignore You

TRUTH: God doesn't disconnect from you. He is not afraid of your sin. He doesn't run from it; He runs to it and you. He is not impulsive, 'He is slow to anger'.

"I can never escape from your spirit! I can never get away from your presence! If I go up to heaven, you are there; if I go down to the place of the dead, you are there. If I ride the wings of the morning, if I dwell by the farthest oceans, even there your hand will guide me, and your strength will support me. I could ask the darkness to hide me and the light around me to become night—but even in darkness I cannot hide from you. To you the night shines as bright as day. Darkness and light are both alike to you."

Psalm 139:7–12 (NLT)

I cannot _____ the presence of God

"The Lord is slow to anger, abounding in love and forgiving sin and rebellion."

Numbers 14:18 (NIV)

LIE #3—God Can Withhold From You

TRUTH: God loves you and has promised you life and not just life, but life to the full! He has made a covenant with you and therefore all that He has is yours. God can withhold things for you, but not from you. He gives you His best. God will never punish you by withholding Himself or His presence from you.

"For the Lord God is our sun and our shield. He gives us grace and glory. The Lord will withhold no good thing from those who do what is right."

Psalm 84:11 (NLT)

God withholds _____ _____ _____ from me

♥ LOVE IT

REFLECTION TIME (Personal)

1. How did you first learn about sex and what were your first thoughts about it?

_____

_____

_____

_____

_____

2. When you have questions about sex, where do you go for answers?

_____

_____

_____

_____

_____

_____

3. Have you ever felt like you couldn't talk to God about what's going on inside of you? Why?

_____

_____

_____

_____

_____

CONNECTION QUESTIONS (Small Group)

1. Out of the three environments mentioned in the lesson (silent, saturated and conflicted) which one sounds familiar and why?

_____

_____

_____

_____

_____

_____

2. Out of the three main lies about God (God can reject me, God can ignore me, God can withhold from me) which did you most identify with and why?

_____

_____

_____

_____

_____

3. What one thing most surprised you about God from this lesson and why?

_____

_____

_____

_____

_____

_____

_____

LIVE IT

1. **My life**—Take a moment this week to talk to God about sex. Tell Him what you think about it—everything! For example—what you know, what you're ashamed of, what you like about it. Then write down anything you think God says to you. *It's okay if you don't hear anything right away!*

_____

_____

_____

_____

_____

_____

_____

2. My friends—When your friends start talking about sex, pay attention to how they talk about it and how it makes you feel.

_____

_____

_____

_____

_____

_____

_____

3. My world—Have you ever noticed how much sex sells? Begin to look for this in music, movies, and advertisements.

_____

_____

_____

_____

_____

_____

_____

 **PRAYER**

Take some time to pray together and talk with God about what you have heard, discussed and learned in this lesson. Ask yourself if you have believed lies about who God is. Confess and pray for each other, asking God to reveal his true nature and character to you.

BEYOND THE BOOK

- Take the test at the end of this chapter
- Read the memory verse each day this week
- Watch this couch conversation on the topic of sex

SEX & GOD TEST

	STRONGLY DISAGREE	MOSTLY DISAGREE	SOMEWHAT DISAGREE	AGREE SOMEWHAT	MOSTLY AGREE	STRONGLY AGREE
I know God loves me unconditionally because I experience it as a reality, not just as a truth in the Bible.	1	2	3	4	5	6
I know God loves that I have a sex drive because He gave it to me.	1	2	3	4	5	6
I can dialogue easily with God about my sexuality and sexual desire.	1	2	3	4	5	6
I have a healthy understanding and view of how God sees sex.	1	2	3	4	5	6
I am aware of lies that I believe about God.	1	2	3	4	5	6
I know that God doesn't withhold things from me but FOR me.	1	2	3	4	5	6

CITATIONS

[1]Sex as a Picture of the Inner Life of God by Glenn Stanton: http://www.focusonthefamily.com/marriage/sex_and_intimacy/gods_design_for_sex/inner_life_of_god.aspx

[2]Wendell Berry, Sex Economy, Freedom, and Community (New York: Pantheon Books, 1993) pp. 138–139.

U2 IDENTITY

- God Has a Yes
- You Are a Powerful Person
- With Power Comes Responsibility

 CONNECTION

- If you are using this Student Guide as a small group, share an insight from your journey since last week.

 MEMORY VERSE

"For I know the plans I have for you," says the Eternal, "plans for peace, not evil, to give you a future and hope—never forget that."

Jeremiah 29:11 (VOICE)

LEARN IT

QUESTION: Does God say 'yes' or 'no' to sex?

God's heart is for us to have it all—our desires, our dreams, a great sex life. Everything is a YES, but with boundaries. Because He loves us and we're worth protecting, He only says "no" when we aren't staying within the (protective) boundaries He has set up.

Everything is a _____, but with boundaries.

"God took the Man and set him down in the Garden of Eden to work the ground and keep it in order. God commanded the Man, "You can eat from any tree in the garden, except from the Tree-of-Knowledge-of-Good-and-Evil. Don't eat from it. The moment you eat from that tree, you're dead."
Genesis 2:15–17 (MSG)

QUESTION: Where do your choices come from?

God gives you a choice and that makes you a powerful! Your choices come out of what you believe, so what you believe becomes the most powerful force in your life.

"Today I have given you the choice between life and death, between blessings and curses. Now I call on heaven and earth to witness the choice you make. Oh, that you would choose life, so that you and your descendants might live! You can make this choice by loving the Lord your God, obeying him, and committing yourself firmly to him."
Deuteronomy 30:18–20 (NLT)

QUESTION: Do I Believe God?

I believe God is who He says He is and that He does what He says He'll do.

"God is not a man, so he does not lie. He is not human, so he does not change his mind. Has he ever spoken and failed to act? Has he ever promised and not carried it through?"
Numbers 23:18 (NLT)

"So God has given both his promise and his oath. These two things are unchangeable because it is impossible for God to lie."

Hebrews 6:18a (NLT)

It is _____ for God to lie.

God wants us to have it all—a full life, healthy relationships, a fruitful marriage, and a fulfilling sex life. He created sex between a man and a woman, and everything He creates is good.

"For everything God created is good, and nothing is to be rejected if it is received with thanksgiving."

1 Timothy 4:4 (NIV)

_____ God created is good.

QUESTION: Do I Trust God?

I believe God can be trusted because He is consistent and always gives me His best.

"Jesus Christ is the same yesterday and today and forever."

Hebrews 13:8 (NIV)

God is _____.

"He who did not spare his own Son, but gave him up for us all—how will he not also, along with him, graciously give us all things."

Romans 8:32 (NIV)

God sees the whole picture. Therefore, I trust His perspective and advice because He sees things that I have yet to experience or understand.

"The Lord himself goes before you and will be with you; he will never leave you or forsake you. Do not be afraid; do not be discouraged."
Deuteronomy 31:8 (NIV)

God sees the _____ picture of my life.
I believe God can be trusted because He is consistent and always gives me His best.

"Jesus Christ is the same yesterday and today and forever."
Hebrews 13:8 (NIV)

God is _____.

"He who did not spare his own Son, but gave him up for us all—how will he not also, along with him, graciously give us all things."
Romans 8:32 (NIV)

God sees the whole picture. Therefore, I trust His perspective and advice because He sees things that I have yet to experience or understand.

"The Lord himself goes before you and will be with you; he will never leave you or forsake you. Do not be afraid; do not be discouraged."
Deuteronomy 31:8 (NIV)

God sees the _____ picture of my life.

QUESTION: Do I Believe I Am Powerful?
I believe, with God's help, there is nothing I can't do.

"I can do everything through Him who gives me strength."
Philippians 4:13 (NIV)

With God's help, there is _____ I can't do.

God's Spirit gives us the ability and the power to manage our lives in any given situation.

"Today I have given you the choice between life and death, between blessings and curses. Now I call on heaven and earth to witness the choice you make. Oh, that you would choose life, so that you and your descendants might live! You can make this choice by loving the LORD your God, obeying him, and committing yourself firmly to him. This is the key to your life."
Deuteronomy 30:19–20 (NLT)

Therefore, regardless of person or circumstance, I am responsible for my decisions and choices. If I made poor decisions in the past, my past does not define my future, God does.

"So let's get this clear: it's for My own sake that I save you. I am He who wipes the slate clean and erases your wrongdoing. I will not call to mind your sins anymore."
Isaiah 43:25 (VOICE)

My past does not _____ my future.

QUESTION: Am I Honorable?

I believe that every person, including myself, is due and worthy of honor because we are all made in His image. For that reason I will honor you, not because of your titles or choices, but because I am honorable.

"Do nothing out of selfish ambition or vain conceit. Rather, in humility value others above yourselves."
Philippians 2:3 (NIV)

I will _____ you because I am _____.

God chose me before the foundation of the earth and paid a high price to display himself through me. Therefore, I choose to honor myself and my body by protecting what has been entrusted to me by a loving Father.

"...you were bought at a price. Therefore honor God with your bodies."
1 Corinthians 6:20 (NIV)

I will _____ what has been entrusted to me.

QUESTION: Do I Believe I Am Significant?

God writes great stories full of redemption and adventure, and I must believe He is excited to write mine as well. Because He uniquely created me with intention, detail, and purpose, the role I play in His story is vital and irreplaceable.

"And who knows but that you have come to your royal position for such a time as this?"
Esther 4:14 (NIV)

Esther was pivotal to the saving of her nation. You are being invited into a story of unique significance. Your life is not just about you, but those people that you will impact and influence.

God _____ created me with _____,

detail and purpose.

Look at Moses, David & Peter. They all messed up, had encounters with God and through their restoration and redemption became significant leaders that impacted the masses. You have never messed up 'too much' and it's never too late to re-engage with the journey he has you on.

"..all the days ordained for me were written in your book before one of them came to be."
Psalm 139:16 (NIV)

My story is full of redemption and adventure!

 **LOVE IT**

REFLECTION TIME (Personal)

1. The word honor means 'great respect; high esteem.' Do you view and treat yourself like this? If not, take a moment to ask God what it is that is clouding your vision and preventing you from valuing yourself.

_____

_____

_____

_____

_____

2. When you think about God's boundaries, do you find you want to rebel, argue or submit? Be honest with yourself and Him. Are you believing a lie about what He's like?

_____

_____

_____

_____

_____

3. Are you living in your own small story, thinking just about how your actions affect you, or are you daring to believe that you are called to influence many and that your choices for integrity matter (when no-one but God is looking)?

_____

_____

_____

_____

_____

_____

CONNECTION QUESTIONS (Small Group)

1. Are you able to say 'yes' to God when He sets a boundary or is it a struggle? Discuss this; be vulnerable to share why or perhaps why you aren't in some areas.

_____

_____

_____

_____

_____

_____

2. What does it mean to be powerful and yet submitted at the same time? Discuss.

_____

_____

_____

_____

_____

_____

3. Have you 'blown it' recently? Know that Jesus totally empathizes with your weakness and is full of redemption. Confess to Him, confess to each other and encourage each other.

_____

_____

_____

_____

_____

_____

◻ LIVE IT

1. **My life**—Take time this week to determine and reflect on the 5 power beliefs.

_____

_____

_____

_____

_____

_____

2. **My friends**—Find a group of trustworthy friends that have similar beliefs and can help hold you accountable to these beliefs.

_____

_____

_____

_____

_____

3. **My world**—In your daily life, ask yourself what is currently influencing your beliefs? (eg. media, church, peers, parents, government, etc.) Have you chosen them for yourself?

_____

_____

_____

_____

PRAYER

Take some time to talk with God. If you need to repent of (turn your thoughts and focus away from) anything then do so. Read Psalm 51 and then talk with Him about re-engaging in your journey together. Thank Him for His mercies, which are new every morning (Lamentations 3:22–23) and make a new commitment to live by the 5 power beliefs. Own your new responsibility and start using the 5 Power Beliefs as your daily declarations.

★ BEYOND THE BOOK

- Take the test at the end of this chapter
- Read the memory verse each day this week
- Watch this Real Story video

SEX & IDENTITY TEST

	STRONGLY DISAGREE	MOSTLY DISAGREE	SOMEWHAT DISAGREE	AGREE SOMEWHAT	MOSTLY AGREE	STRONGLY AGREE
I am managing my choices within the boundaries God sets as this is necessary for me to grow in freedom.	1	2	3	4	5	6
I believe that God wants to give me good things because He has said so and He cannot lie.	1	2	3	4	5	6
I trust God and His perspective on my life because He sees the big picture.	1	2	3	4	5	6
I believe that with God's help there is nothing I cannot do.	1	2	3	4	5	6
I am treating the opposite sex and their bodies with honor and value because I am honorable.	1	2	3	4	5	6
My choices for integrity matter because I am daring to believe I am called to influence many.	1	2	3	4	5	6

03 SEX & THE BODY PART ONE

- Body, Soul & Spirit
- Part 1: The Body—Functions and Needs

 CONNECTION

- Share any revelations you got this past week either as a result of doing the lesson or from additional reading or watching that you did.

MEMORY VERSE

"But don't think you've preserved your virtue simply by staying out of bed. Your heart can be corrupted by lust even quicker than your body."

Matthew 5:27–28 (MSG)

 LEARN IT

QUESTION: Is sex just a physical experience?

We are made up of three parts: body, soul (mind, will & emotions) and spirit.

"Now may the God of peace Himself sanctify you entirely; and may your spirit and soul and body be preserved complete, without blame at the coming of our Lord Jesus Christ."

1 Thessalonians 5:23

You cannot separate the 'parts' of yourself any more than you can separate God from you!

"Haven't you read in your Bible that the Creator originally made man and woman for each other, male and female? And because of this, a man leaves his father and mother and is firmly bonded to his wife, becoming one flesh—no longer two bodies but one. Because God created this organic union of the two sexes, no one should desecrate His art by cutting them apart."

Matthew 19:4–6 (MSG)

God created sex to be more than a physical experience; it is a multi-dimensional experience. When we have sex we are connecting at all levels: body, soul and spirit.

Sex creates a connection at the _____,

_____ and _____ levels.

QUESTION: What happens when we have sex?

Sex is intercourse between two people—vaginal, anal and oral. At the point of arousal endorphins and hormones are released, making sex enjoyable, bonding and addictive.

During arousal the 'reason and behavior control center' shuts down in our brains and the brain becomes governed by the cerebral cortex—the part of the brain responsible for memory. *Memories are built during sex.*

This explains why our thoughts are overtaken and we never forget the people we have sex with.

_____ are built during sex.

QUESTION: What's happening at a biological level?

Certain chemical reactions are going on in our bodies as we engage in sex. Chemicals are released that have an effect on our bodies and emotions.

1. **Endorphins (Dopamine and Serotonin)**—the "happy" chemicals
   - These chemicals cause an intense rush of pleasure.
   - They sharpen our ability to focus and concentrate.
   - Dopamine is also known as the "reward" hormone, releasing pleasure and a desire to repeat the activity.

2. **Oxytocin**—the "trust and pair-bonding" hormone
   - This hormone is what causes you to feel deeply bonded or attached. (It is also released between a mother and her child when the child is born.)
   - It eases stress, creating feelings of "calm and closeness," which leads to increased trust. Women, in general, have a stronger reaction to oxytocin, than men.
   - It also crystallizes emotional memories in our minds, making sex with another person very hard to forget.

3. **Vasopressin**—the "commitment" hormone
   - This hormone generates the desire to commit to our mate.
   - It inspires loyalty and arouses jealousy in a man towards a woman he's had sex with.
   - It also drives us to protect our territory and offspring; heightening our sense of responsibility.

"...studies reveal the rationale behind an inability of some to stay bonded in seemingly good relationships. People who have misused sex to become bonded with multiple persons will diminish their oxytocin bonding within their current relationship. In the absence of oxytocin, the person will find less or no excitement. The person will, then, feel the need to move on to what looks more exciting."[1]

"Sex, whether you want it to or not, connects you on every level with another person—spirit to spirit, soul to soul and body to body."[2]

QUESTION: Are there levels of intimacy?

We are looking at three levels: looking, thinking and touching.

Our bodies all respond to different levels of stimuli. Whether it's touching, looking at, or simply thinking about the opposite sex, you are creating intimacy that you will pattern throughout your life.

Looking—Lusting

Lust is defined as an overwhelming or intense desire or craving. It destroys our ability to love by making us selfish.

- Love is about giving yourself to another person
- Lust is about taking from another for self-satisfaction
- Looking can hurt us

"You know the next commandment pretty well, too: 'Don't go to bed with another's spouse.' But don't think you've preserved your virtue simply by staying out of bed. Your heart can be corrupted by lust even quicker than your body. Those leering looks you think nobody notices— they also corrupt."

Matthew 5:27–28 (MSG)

Looking can _____ us.

Thinking—Fantasizing
Fantasizing is defined as "indulging your thinking about something you desire". When we direct our fantasization towards a 'someone' it begins to take us down a road of unreality.

Our fantasies can give our lives a false sense of meaning and we can often end up fantasizing to fill a deeper void. Our thoughts are very powerful.

"For as he thinks in his heart, so is he..."
Proverbs 23:7 (AMP)

Our thoughts are very _____.

Our thoughts can also determine our actions. In other words, if we think about something for long enough, our behaviour will change and we will be tempted to take steps to make our thoughts a reality.

"Be careful what you think, because your thoughts run your life."
Proverbs 4:23 (NCV)

Our thoughts can determine our _____.

Touching
Touching is defined as "to come so close to something as to be or come into contact with". From holding hands to sexual intercourse; all and any physical contact and interaction you have with another person will release some level of chemical response in your body.

The goal is to recognise what is going on and learn your own point of arousal.

"I charge you not to excite your love until it is ready. Don't stir a fire in your heart too soon, until it is ready to be satisfied."

Song of Solomon 8:4 (VOICE)

Taking responsibility for our own sex drives is critical and no one can draw your "purity line" for you. Remember that God will always be pursuing our hearts rather than controlling our behaviour.

God created sex to bond a husband and a wife (within the boundaries of marital covenant) physically, emotionally (soul), and spiritually.

 ## LOVE IT

REFLECTION TIME (Personal)

1. Have you had a previous sexual experience (sexual encounter, pornography, masturbation, etc.) that left you with a 'pulling' connection? Don't worry, there is nothing wrong with you! It's normal to feel bonded. Take a moment and invite the Holy Spirit into the experience. Ask Him to help you break any unhealthy connection that exists.

_____

_____

_____

_____

_____

2. Do you find yourself fantasizing (sexual, romantic or non-sexual) in order to fill a deeper void? How can you invite God into this area of your life and allow Him to fill the voids?

_____

_____

_____

_____

_____

_____

CONNECTION QUESTIONS (Small Group)

1. Is it a new concept for you to think your sex drive is given to you by God? Does this at all change your view on sex?

_____

_____

_____

_____

_____

2. Have you used your power of choice when it comes to your purity this year? Give an example.

_____

_____

_____

_____

3. As we've talked about sex being a body, soul and spirit experience, have you noticed this to be true in your life? If not in your own life, have you noticed it in a friend's life?

_____

_____

_____

_____

_____

_____

LIVE IT

1. **My life**—We've talked about your God-given ability to create your own 'purity line'. Take a moment this week and invite God to show you yours. Make sure you get a chance to write it down.

_____

_____

_____

_____

_____

_____

2. My friends—Find one or two trustworthy friends (mentors, youth leaders, etc.) to hold you accountable to your purity line, whether you are single or in a relationship.

_____

_____

_____

_____

_____

_____

3. My world—Pay attention to how the world displays its view on sex (media, movies, advertisements, etc.) and compare it to the truth of what you've learned about sex in this lesson.

_____

_____

_____

 **PRAYER**

All of your being is involved in sex and sex affects all of you. You can't separate your body from your soul and spirit. Ask God to separate you from people and experiences if you need to. Pray for one another.

★ BEYOND THE BOOK

- Take the test at the end of this chapter
- Read the memory verse each day this week
- Listen to this podcast on Kingdom Sexuality
- Read this article

SEX & THE BODY TEST —PART 1

	STRONGLY DISAGREE	MOSTLY DISAGREE	SOMEWHAT DISAGREE	AGREE SOMEWHAT	MOSTLY AGREE	STRONGLY AGREE
God gave me the power and responsibility to make choices so that I could experience freedom.	1	2	3	4	5	6
There are things I don't do with, or to my body because I consider my body valuable & holy.	1	2	3	4	5	6
My body's capacity for sex is a powerful thing. I am using that capacity constructively.	1	2	3	4	5	6
God won't control my sex drive for me, but I am inviting His help in my learning how to control it.	1	2	3	4	5	6
I am aware of what's going on when I fantasize and am seeking to take 'every thought captive'.	1	2	3	4	5	6
I am fully aware of my own point of arousal and am managing myself accordingly.	1	2	3	4	5	6

CITATIONS

[1]http://thenewviewonsex.blogspot.com/2008/04/oxytocin-vasopressin-and-tale-of-two.html

[2]Moral Revolution 40 Day Journey to Purity: Girls p.169

04 SEX & THE BODY PART TWO

- Body, Soul & Spirit Review
- Part 2: Basic Human Needs: Body—Soul—Spirit
- Living from Our Spirit

 ## CONNECTION

- Ask if anyone in the group has a testimony of how doing this course is changing them.

 ## MEMORY VERSE

"There is more to sex than mere skin to skin... We must not pursue the kind of sex that avoids commitment and intimacy, leaving us more lonely than ever—the kind of sex that can never "become one."

1 Corinthians 6:16–18 (MSG)

LEARN IT

THE BODY
The body is made up of our flesh and bones and also our 5 senses—touch, sight, hearing, smell and taste.

In order to physically survive our human body needs food, water, air, shelter and human contact.

Abuse of these needs (due to excess or lack) can lead to physical illness, obesity, anorexia or death (This is true of newborns going without physical contact[1]).

Abuse of my body needs can lead to _____

_____, _____,

_____ or _____.

THE SOUL

The soul is the realm of every emotion we feel, every thought we think and every desire or appetite we are driven by.

"How lovely is your dwelling place, Lord Almighty! My soul yearns, even faints, for the courts of the Lord; my heart and my flesh cry out for the living God."

Psalm 84:1–2 (NIV)

In order to emotionally survive our soul needs intimacy, connection and comfort.

"You who are my Comforter in sorrow, my heart is faint within me."

Jeremiah 8:18 (NIV)

Our soul needs are affected and met, to a degree, by our body and spirit. Remember the chemicals we said get released and cause an emotional connection? Well it isn't only sex that releases these, there are other activities that we can do that cause a release of the 'feel-good' chemicals.

Some other things that cause the release of the 'feel-good' chemicals _____

_____.

Abuse of our soul needs either looks like:

- Trying to get them met through physical activity, which can lead to addiction or
- Shutting down our emotions all together and leaving ourselves in a place where there is nothing that is able influence or stimulate the 'feel-good' factor in our lives.

Abuse of my soul needs can lead to _____ or

_____ my emotions.

Our spirit also affects and meets the needs of our soul through connection with God.

"My soul yearns for you in the night; in the morning my spirit longs for you."
Isaiah 26:9 (NIV)

Our body and our spirit were created to healthily affect our soul. Because physical resources are limited, the key is allowing our spirit to be the primary source of meeting our soul needs.

The key to getting our soul needs met in a healthy way is

allowing our _____ to be the primary source.

SPIRIT

The spirit part of us is our place of deepest connection with God and where His Spirit lives in us.

"You, however, are not in the realm of the flesh but are in the realm of the Spirit, if indeed the Spirit of God lives in you."
Romans 8:9 (NIV)

In order to spiritually thrive we need one thing and one thing only: God!

"But when you are joined with the Lord, you become one spirit with Him."
1 Corinthians 6:17 (VOICE)

Abuse of our spiritual needs looks like idolatry. That is, anything that we put in our 'God-spot' that meets our need for identity.

We know we are getting our identity need met here if something happens to remove us from that place and we find that we no longer know who we are.

Abuse of my spiritual needs means something else is

giving me _____.

QUESTION: *Who is in charge of my life? My body, soul or spirit?*

When we are born-again we get connected us to the One that is willing and able to meet ALL our needs.

"Know this: my God will also fill every need you have according to His glorious riches in Jesus."
Philippians 4:19 (VOICE)

God will _____ every need I have.

Engaging with Him and allowing our spirit to be in charge, is a choice. If we do not do this, the Bible says we are vulnerable to attack.

"He who has no rule over his own spirit is like a city that is broken down and without walls."
Proverbs 25:28 (AMP)

If I don't exercise self-control (allow my spirit to lead my

will) I am _____ to attack.

Being born again means that God has given us the capacity to manage our thoughts, appetites and behaviour.

"For God did not give us a spirit of timidity.. but He has given us a spirit of power and of love and of calm and well-balanced mind and discipline and self-control."
2 Timothy 1:7 (AMP)

Our soul (mind, emotions and will) responds directly to whatever we are feeding on.

"For as he thinks in his heart, so is he…"
Proverbs 23:7 (AMP)

My soul is affected by what I am _____ on.

When we are living Spirit-led lives (ie. in relationship with and listening to the Holy Spirit) our thoughts, emotions, and desires begin to reflect His—and become healthy and holy.

"As water reflects the face, so one's life reflects the heart." Proverbs 27:19 (NIV)

When we are not living Spirit-led lives, and are getting our soul needs met from other sources, our thoughts, emotions and desires become toxic and destructive and can lead to addictive behaviours.

When I am not living a Spirit-led life, my thoughts,

emotions and desires become _____

and _____.

The answer to getting our deepest needs met is through close, intimate, personal relationship with Jesus.

God has made us in such a way that our body, our soul and our spirit are inter-connected and our health (or lack of it) in one area, affects the other two areas.

If we do not acknowledge our soul needs or ignore them, we will find ourselves in danger of forming comfort habits such as overeating, pornography etc. This is where addressing the needs of our spirit becomes vital.

Addressing the needs of my spirit is _____.

Constant connection with God establishes identity and allows us to be completely seen and known. This relationship with Him is the only way to get our deepest needs met.

 **LOVE IT**

REFLECTION TIME (Personal)

1. Do you find yourself ignoring one or all of these areas of need? Body (physical needs), soul (emotional feelings), or spirit (talking to God) needs? What can you do differently to make sure all of these needs are getting met in a healthy way?

_____

_____

_____

_____

_____

2. You are in a process of learning to understand your needs and desires and developing healthy skills for meeting them. Along this journey, it's totally normal to make mistakes. How do you currently handle your mistakes? Do you punish yourself? Do you talk about it in community?

_____

_____

_____

_____

_____

_____

CONNECTION QUESTIONS (Small Group)

1. What are 2 or 3 things you can implement in your life to begin or maintain constant connection with God to ensure you are living from your spirit (ie. bringing your needs under the covering and rule of your spirit)?

_____

_____

_____

_____

_____

2. Do you recognize any areas in your life where you are abusing external resources to try to get your needs met? If so, what can you do differently to manage those needs?

_____

_____

_____

_____

_____

3. What does it look like to live as a triune (body, soul, spirit) being?

_____

_____

_____

_____

_____

 **LIVE IT**

1. **My life**—This week, find ways to connect with each part of your being (body, soul, spirit). For example, spend time with the Lord to meet the needs of you spirit. Go for a walk, or exercise to help meet the needs of your physical body. Hang out with your closest friends or watch a funny movie to fulfill your soul needs.

_____

_____

_____

_____

_____

_____

2. **My friends**—Challenge your friends this week to bring their full selves to the table in your conversations. Find out how this will affect not only your personal life, but also your friendships. Then relate this to being a healthy body, soul and spirit.

_____

_____

_____

_____

_____

_____

3. My world—Observe the world around you, whether it be school, your family, or TV shows, and notice how they fulfill their needs when they are feeling alone or frustrated. Compare that to what you learned this week.

_____

_____

_____

 PRAYER

It's so important to acknowledge that you are a triune being. Take some time with Jesus to talk about your emotions, your thoughts and your will. Thank Him that He took time on earth to live as a man so that He would know exactly what you are dealing with. Make a fresh commitment to trust Him and bring all your needs to Him. Ask Him to reveal where you might be using a legitimate external source (such as TV, sport, recreation) abusively (ie. to meet a need).

BEYOND THE BOOK

- Take the test at the end of this chapter
- Read the memory verse each day this week
- Watch this video on needs

SEX & THE BODY TEST PART 2

	STRONGLY DISAGREE	MOSTLY DISAGREE	SOMEWHAT DISAGREE	AGREE SOMEWHAT	MOSTLY AGREE	STRONGLY AGREE
I love my body. It is a valuable gift from God.	1	2	3	4	5	6
When I am sad, lonely or in pain, I am aware that I have a choice of who or what I look to for comfort & relief.	1	2	3	4	5	6
I try to be raw and real with God about what is going on inside me.	1	2	3	4	5	6
I think of myself as a spirit, soul & body and understand that my choices involve every aspect of my being.	1	2	3	4	5	6
I am quick to recognize when I am abusing a legitimate external source (eg. food) to get my 'comfort' need met.	1	2	3	4	5	6
I don't look to anything else (eg. clothes, sport, music, friends) to get my need for identity met. Instead I look to God to tell me who I am and how loved I am.	1	2	3	4	5	6

CITATIONS
[1]Coila, B. (2013, Aug 13). The effect of human contact on newborn babies. Retrieved from http://www.livestrong.com/article/72120-effect-human-contact-newborn-babies/

05 SEX & RESTORATION

- Spirit Restoration
- Soul (Mind, Will & Emotions) Restoration
- Body (Physical) Restoration

CONNECTION

- Share with each other what are learning on this journey, including any breakthroughs you have had in any area.

MEMORY VERSE

"Create in me a pure heart, O God, and renew a steadfast spirit within me.... Restore to me the joy of your salvation and grant me a willing spirit to sustain me."

Psalm 51:10–12 (NIV)

LEARN IT

QUESTION: What do we mean by 'restoration'?

The dictionary defines restoration as "the action of returning something to a former condition; of reinstating it back to its original form or function."

After his sexual sin, King David wrote Psalm 51 to God:

"Create in me a pure heart, O God, and renew a steadfast spirit within me…. Restore to me the joy of your salvation and grant me a willing spirit, to sustain me."

The Hebrew root word for renew and restore is the verb 'chadash', meaning to renew oneself, repair, restore or even to polish a sword until it gleams!

The root word for steadfast is 'niphal' meaning to be firm, stable and established; securely determined, enduring.

We are saying "Lord, renew my ability to be determined and restore my shine!"

SPIRIT RESTORATION
Premarital sex affects our spirit, because it's a sin; against God and our own body.

"Against you, you only, have I sinned and done what is evil in your sight."
Psalm 51:4a (NIV)

"Flee from sexual immorality. All other sins a person commits are outside the body, but whoever sins sexually, sins against their own body."
1 Corinthians 6:18 (NIV)

Premarital sex is a sin against _____ and against

my _____.

In the Old Testament when the Israelites sinned, it separated them from God and only offerings and sacrifices reconnected them.

Before we believed in Jesus, our sin separated us from God.

"...remember that at that time you were separate from Christ, excluded from citizenship... and foreigners to the covenants of the promise,without hope and without God in the world."

Ephesians 2:12 (NIV)

The good news is that Jesus made the 'one time' sacrifice for us, to pay for our sin.

"He is not like the other priests who had to offer sacrifices every day, first for their own sins, and then for the sins of the people. Christ offered his sacrifice only once and for all time when he offered himself."

Hebrews 7:27 (NCV)

Jesus made a _____ _____ sacrifice for my sin.

It is impossible for God to separate himself from us once we have chosen to believe in Jesus.

"..nothing above us, nothing below us, nor anything else in the whole world will ever be able to separate us from the love of God that is in Christ Jesus our Lord."

Romans 8:39 (NCV)

_____ can separate me from the love of God.

However, our sin does affect our fellowship with God.

When we choose to sin we turn our backs on God and when we do that, we feel disconnected so we believe we are, when in fact He hasn't moved.

The lies we believed that caused us to sin are not unlike those that Adam & Eve believed, and our resulting behavior is the same.

We Don't Believe Him
We question who God is; His nature and His character.

"Did God really say...?"
Genesis 3:1 (NIV)

We doubt and waver in our belief.

We Replace Him
Satan will tell us that intimacy with God is not enough.

When we go to something or someone else to get our deepest need for identity, intimacy, significance etc. met, then we are replacing Him and are committing adultery or idolatry.

"They consult their wooden idols....The wind of prostitution blows them astray; they commit spiritual adultery against their God."
Hosea 4:12 (NET)

When I go to something or someone to get my deepest

needs met, I am committing _____ or

_____.

We Hide From Him

We believe God separates Himself from us because we think He is afraid of or can't handle our sin. We are full of shame.

"Then the eyes of both of them were opened, and they realized they were naked; so they sewed fig leaves together and made coverings for themselves ...and they hid from the Lord God."

Genesis 3:7–8b (NIV)

Repentance instantly restores our connection with God, because we are turning back to Him.

The original Greek word for repentance is metanoia, which means: "'change of mind' and involves a turning with remorse from sin to God with a hatred for and disgust of one's sins."[1]

"I correct and train those I love. So be sincere, and turn away from your sins."

Revelation 3:19 (NIRV)

As we simply turn our thoughts to Him, He responds immediately and we are reconnected.

"Come near to God and he will come near to you. Wash your hands, you sinners, and purify your hearts, you double-minded.... Humble yourselves before the Lord, and he will lift you up."

James 4:8–10 (NIV)

God responds to my 'turning'_____.

God is ready and wanting to forgive us and restore our spirit connection with Him.

"If we confess our sins, he is faithful and just and will forgive us our sins."
1 John 1:9 (NIV)

Extravagant forgiveness is God's idea and forgiveness restores the standard.

SOUL (MIND, WILL & EMOTIONS) RESTORATION

MIND
Premarital sex changes the way you think about yourself and the way you view the world. You can be left believing some lies:

e.g. I am not worth the wait, the commitment, or the protection.

e.g. I am a victim to my hormones and temptations.

e.g. I'll never get married; marriage doesn't last.

God says that the truth will set you free; therefore, it is vital that we know the Word of God.

"Then you will know the truth, and the truth will set you free."
John 8:32 (NIV)

Knowing the truth sets me _____.

The Bible instructs us to take our thoughts 'captive' and to renew our minds.

As we do this, we will start changing the way we live. Renewing our minds will lead to transformation

"Do not conform to the pattern of this world, but be transformed by the renewing of your mind."
Romans 12:2 (NIV)

Renewing my mind will lead to _____.

WILL
Premarital sex looks desirable when we don't understand its effect.

The enemy is a deceiver destroyer and a liar! Therefore, anything he is tempting us with can only result in destruction.

"...the thief comes only to steal, and kill and destroy."
John 10:10a (NIV)

Anything the enemy tempts me with will result in

_____.

Jesus understands what you are facing because He was tempted in every way!

"For we do not have a high priest who is unable to empathize with our weaknesses, but we have one who has been tempted in every way, just as we are—yet he did not sin."
Hebrews 4:15 (NIV)

Jesus fully _____ with my weaknesses.

There is no temptation that we can't overcome and God has promised us that he will ALWAYS give us a way out!

"No temptation has overtaken you except what is common to mankind. And God is faithful; he will not let you be tempted beyond what you can bear. But when you are tempted, he will also provide a way out so that you can endure it."
1 Corinthians 10:13 (NIV)

There is _____ temptation I can't overcome because God

will _____ provide a way out.

EMOTIONS
Premarital sex affects our soul by keeping us unhealthily attached to people we are not in covenant with. We call this an unhealthy soul-tie.

A soul-tie is defined as: the emotional bond between two people created through time investment, life exchange, and commitment.

A soul-tie is an _____ _____

between two people.

Soul-ties are healthy when they involve covenant and commitment. An example of healthy soul-tie is the one between David and Jonathan.

"Jonathan was deeply impressed with David—an immediate bond was forged between them."

1 Samuel 18:1 (MSG)

Soul-ties are healthy when they involve _____

and _____.

Sex outside marriage is forbidden and therefore creates an unhealthy soul-tie.

"There's more to sex than mere skin on skin. Sex is as much spiritual mystery as physical fact. As written in Scripture, "The two become one.""
1 Corinthians 6:16 (MSG)

Sex outside of marriage creates an _____

soul-tie.

BODY (PHYSICAL) RESTORATION

When we have sex our physical body is affected. Chemicals are released and our brains build "muscle memory" (synapses) causing us to want to repeat the behavior.

Scientists tell us that our brain's muscle memory is moldable from before birth until after death![2] So if we starve it of familiar thoughts, the muscle memory begins to wither and die.

In addition to our body's ability to self-heal; God heals supernaturally!

"People brought anybody with an ailment, whether mental, emotional, or physical. Jesus healed them, one and all."
Matt 4:24 (MSG)

God is willing and able to take any of your mistakes and restore you, spirit, soul and body.

"And we know that in all things God works for the good of those who love him, who have been called according to his purpose."
Romans 8:28 (NIV)

There is _____ part of me or my life that God cannot restore.

 **LOVE IT**

REFLECTION TIME (Personal)

1. Take some time and ask the Holy Spirit to reveal to you whether you are dealing with shame in any area of your life. Is it causing (or has it caused) you to hide from Him?

_____

_____

_____

_____

_____

_____

2. Is there any area in your life that you want made new/restored? If so, start dialoguing with God about it. Is there anything you need to talk to Him about and ask forgiveness for (repent)?

_____

_____

_____

_____

_____

_____

_____

3. Is there a destructive habit that you are dealing with? Having heard the information on scientific and supernatural hope for change, are you encouraged to know that you can partner with the Holy Spirit to strengthen your will to bring freedom? Ask the Lord to show you the hope He has for you in that area. Spend some time thanking God for this.

_____

_____

_____

_____

_____

_____

_____

CONNECTION QUESTIONS (Small Group)

1. Were you aware of the power that God has to restore/ heal all of your being? How do you feel about the restoration process that was discussed in this lesson? Discuss with one another.

_____

_____

_____

_____

_____

2. Do you have habits or behaviors that you want to change? Do you feel like you can talk to God about them? Talk within the group or in pairs about why this might be.

_____

_____

_____

_____

3. What can you do now to start taking steps to break old habits and establish new behaviors? Who can you share this with? Who can encourage you in your process?

_____

_____

_____

_____

 **LIVE IT**

1. **My life**—Take time this week to journal and think about who you want to be in 10 years. What do you want to be known for? What theme is your story going to be shouting to the earth? Hope? Restoration? Overcoming? Purity? Justice? (etc.) Share this with one person in your life. Share this with the Lord and ask Him to give you the hope, courage and strength you need to become that person.

_____

_____

_____

_____

_____

_____

2. **My friends**—Ask two friends in your small group how they are doing with their action plan. Call your mentor and connect at least once to let them know how you are doing.

_____

_____

_____

_____

_____

_____

3. My world—Find stories of people who have overcome in the areas that are covered in this lesson. (You can checkout www.moralrevolution.com for encouraging stories). Note how they did it.

_____

_____

_____

_____

_____

⚜ PRAYER

Repent of any sexual sin. If necessary renounce and break any unhealthy soul-ties you may have formed. Eg, "In Jesus' name, I renounce any ungodly soul ties formed between myself and _____ as a result of _____ (pre-marital sex, etc)." and "I break and sever any ungodly soul ties formed between myself and_____ as a result of _____ in Jesus' name. Renounce any rash vows you made. (eg: "I will love you forever!")

Ask God to remove any curse spoken over you by anyone you were in relationship with. (eg: "No man will ever love you the way I love you!"). Spend time thanking Jesus that He paid for everything, once and for all and He will work EVERYTHING you've been through for good.

★ BEYOND THE BOOK

- Take the test at the end of this chapter
- Read the memory verse each day this week
- Watch this Real Story video

- Watch this Real Story video

- Listen to this podcast:
  The Father Who Restores

- Listen to this podcast:
  From The Battlefield to the Bedroom

SEX & RESTORATION TEST

	STRONGLY DISAGREE	MOSTLY DISAGREE	SOMEWHAT DISAGREE	AGREE SOMEWHAT	MOSTLY AGREE	STRONGLY AGREE
When I act beneath my identity, I don't deny it or stuff it. I own up to it before God and let Him remove my shame.	1	2	3	4	5	6
When God looks at me He doesn't see my mistakes. He sees Jesus.	1	2	3	4	5	6
Sexual sin cannot disqualify me from experiencing God's best for my sex life, if I receive restoration.	1	2	3	4	5	6
I want to be willing to give up anything, no matter how good, in order to receive God's best for me.	1	2	3	4	5	6
I was never made to live in secret and in silence; I was made to speak up and freely share who I am.	1	2	3	4	5	6
God makes me 100% pure, inside and out when I repent.	1	2	3	4	5	6

CITATIONS

[1]http://www.blueletterbible.org/lang/lexicon/lexicon.cfm?Strongs=G3340&t=NIV

[2]"Hooked"—by Joe S. McIlhaney, JR., MD & Freda McKissic Bush, MD (page 29)

UU COVENANT

- Do You Have What It Takes? (Covenant)
- Where Are You Going? (Purity Looks Like Something)
- How Are You Going to Get There? (Purity Plan)

CONNECTION

- Last week was a significant lesson.
  Share with each other about how it impacted you.

MEMORY VERSE

"I can do all things through Christ, because he gives me strength."

Philippians 4:13 (NCV)

LEARN IT

QUESTION: What do we mean by covenant?

The definition of covenant is: "a usually formal, solemn, and binding agreement."[1]

It is a binding promise made between two people. It ties you together with another person.

These people are in such close relationship that all they have or possess in this life is available to each other upon request.[2]

A covenant is a _____ _____ made between two people.

Covenant is how God establishes relationship.

Do You Have What It Takes?

Making choices to modify our behaviour and using our will are necessary, but we need God.

His grace and power are available to us when we are in covenant relationship with Him.

"He said to me, "My grace is enough to cover and sustain you. My power is made perfect in weakness.""
2 Corinthians 12:9a (VOICE)

God's _____ and _____ are available to me because we are in covenant.

OLD TESTAMENT COVENANT: GOD AND ABRAHAM (GENESIS 15–17)

God told Abraham to kill an animal and use its blood to represent His and Abraham shed his own blood through physical circumcision.

"You are to undergo circumcision, and it will be the sign of the covenant between me and you."

Genesis 17:11 (NIV)

God made a covenant with Abraham and the whole Israelite nation.

"I will be your God, you will be My people."

Jeremiah 7:23 (NIV)

God had access to His people and Israelites had access to His strength, protection and presence.

NEW TESTAMENT COVENANT: JESUS AND ME (AND THE CHURCH)

"...everything is purified in connection with blood; without the shedding of blood, sin cannot be forgiven."

Hebrews 9:22b (VOICE)

Jesus made covenant with us using His own blood.
We make covenant through circumcision of our hearts.

"In Him you were also circumcised, set apart by a spiritual act performed without hands. The Anointed One's circumcision cut you off from the sinfulness of your flesh."

Colossians 2:11 (VOICE)

My covenant with God is through _____ of

my heart.

Being in covenant with God is about being in such a close relationship with him that:

- everything He has or possesses in this life is available to you upon request, and
- everything you have is available to Him upon His request!

"This is why Jesus is the mediator of the new covenant: through His death, He .... has made it possible for all who are called to receive God's promised inheritance."
Hebrews 9:15 (VOICE)

Do You Know Where You're Going?
Purity looks like something. It is reflected in your thoughts and actions.

""I have the right to do anything," you say—but not everything is beneficial. "I have the right to do anything"—but not everything is constructive."
1 Corinthians 10:23 (NIV)

You need vision for what you want purity to look like in your life. This is your goal.

Purity _____ like something.

Without a destination (goal) you won't be very successful in being pure!
Proverbs 29:18 [VOICE]

How Are You Going to Get There?

Now that you have vision and goals for your sexual purity, you need a PLAN!

To make an effective plan, you need to know what your "red-flags" or triggers are.

What were you feeling, thinking about or experiencing BEFORE you made an unhealthy choice? What was going on? This will help you identify what you were feeling.

To make a plan I need to know what my _____

_____ or _____ are.

Needs

We have needs that we are driven to meet. Our unhealthy behaviors are often a result of us trying to meet our needs inappropriately.

Once we've identified our need, we can decide how to meet it in a healthy way, ith God's help.

With God's help I can meet my needs in a

_____ way.

Accountability

It is important to have people to walk with you; to encourage, challenge and ask you good questions.

"Without wise guidance, a nation falls, but victory is certain when there are plenty of wise counselors."
Proverbs 11:14 (VOICE)

Accountability people need to be trustworthy and people you can be gut-level honest with.

These are people who will help you take ACCOUNT for your ABILITY, not punish you.

An accountability person will take _____ for my

_____ to do well.

In conclusion, you need God's resources to be able to walk in purity—spirit, soul and body!

As we grow and learn what we need and how to get it in a healthy way, we will be setting ourselves up for absolute success in our friendships, dating relationships and marriages.

As I grow and learn I am setting myself up for

_____.

 **LOVE IT**

REFLECTION TIME (Personal)

1. Take some time to think about areas in your life you have tried to hide or have withheld from God; areas you do not trust the Lord in; areas He is asking you to surrender. Write them down now.

_____

_____

_____

_____

_____

2. Have an honest conversation with the Lord about the above areas. Tell Him what you are feeling (afraid, mad, embarrassed, confused, lacking faith, powerless, ashamed, etc.). Invite Him into those areas and, if you are ready, surrender them to Him.

_____

_____

_____

_____

_____

_____

3. Reflect on the great price God paid to enter into a covenant relationship with you, Jesus' death on a cross. Do you believe you alone are worth this sacrifice? Take some time to talk to the Lord about these things (optional communion).

_____

_____

_____

_____

_____

_____

CONNECTION QUESTIONS (Small Group)

1. Was anything you learned in this lesson about covenant new? Surprising? Scary? Daunting?

_____

_____

_____

_____

_____

2. What is the difference between a covenant and a promise? Explain.

_____

_____

_____

_____

_____

3. Were you aware that you entered into a covenant with God when you accepted Jesus as your saviour? How does that change your relationship with Him and the decisions that you make?

_____

_____

_____

_____

4. Are you aware that God views/values your (future) marriage covenant as powerfully as his covenant with you? How does that affect your view of marriage?

_____

_____

_____

_____

_____

_____

4. What is your motivation for entering the purity covenant (should you choose to do so)? Who are you doing it for? (Lord,yourself spouse, future children, parents?)

_____

_____

_____

_____

_____

_____

 **LIVE IT**

1. **My life**—Meditate daily on Phil 4:13 which says, "I can do all things through Christ who strengthens me." This week, practice asking the Lord for whatever grace and strength you need throughout the day. Be sure to record/write down your victories this week.

_____

_____

_____

_____

_____

_____

2. **My friends**—Find one married couple in your life that you honor and respect and ask them to share their story with you. Ask them for advice in dating/marriage. Ask them to describe what sacrifice looks like to them (within marriage).

_____

_____

_____

_____

_____

_____

3. My world—Is there anyone in my home I have a relational mess with? Do I owe anyone an apology (ask for forgiveness)? Do I have to forgive anyone? Take time to make right this week anything that can be wrong in your home. Own your mistakes; and start new. Remember God resists the proud and gives grace to the humble.

_____

_____

_____

 **PRAYER**

Take some time thanking Jesus for shedding His own blood in order to bring you into such a fulfilling covenant relationship with God. Take communion as a reminder of His sacrifice. Thank Him that He has ALL the resources available that you need and that He is setting you up to succeed!

BEYOND THE BOOK

- Take the test at the end of this chapter
- Watch this video on Handling Strong Emotions

- Watch this video on intimacy

- Listen to this podcast: From Your Head to Your Heart

- Listen to this podcast: The Art of Self Control

SEX & COVENANT TEST

	STRONGLY DISAGREE	MOSTLY DISAGREE	SOMEWHAT DISAGREE	AGREE SOMEWHAT	MOSTLY AGREE	STRONGLY AGREE
I often try to modify my behaviour without the help and power of God.	1	2	3	4	5	6
I don't let my mistakes define who I am and whose I am.	1	2	3	4	5	6
I understand the difference between a goal and a plan.	1	2	3	4	5	6
Committing to things brings out the best in me.	1	2	3	4	5	6
I know God will not only uphold His end of our covenant but He will give me what I need to uphold my end.	1	2	3	4	5	6
Even though I live in a society of broken covenants I can be someone who honors and keeps my covenant with God and others.	1	2	3	4	5	6

CITATIONS

[1]http://www.merriam-webster.com/dictionary/covenant

[2]Nelson, W. (2003, May 30). Understanding the blood covenant [Online forum comment]. Retrieved from http://www.faithwriters.com/article-details.php?id=4089

[3]Jones, D. W. & Tarwater, J. K. (2005, September 18). Are biblical covenants dissoluble?: toward a theology of marriage Reformed Perspectives Magazine, 7(38), 5-6. Retrieved from http://myseminary.org/articles/dav_jones/th.tarwater.jones.covenants.pdf

Purity Covenant

A covenant is a binding promise made between two people. This kind of promise ties you together with another person. Each person is responsible to fulfill what they have agreed to in the promise. Each person brings their strength to the relationship to make sure the promise is kept. These people are in such close relationship with each other that all they have or possess in this life is available to each other upon request. In Bible times, this kind of promise could only be dissolved if one of the covenanters died. It is a life-long promise that binds you together for one common purpose.

In making a purity covenant, you are making a promise to both yourself and to God. You are in it for life—it can only end if one of you dies! The purpose? For you to be able to live whole and healthy in your sexuality, both now and after you're married. God wants you to be entirely yourself, the way He created you to be—body, soul and spirit—knowing that this will enable you to fully enjoy an intimate marital relationship with the man or woman of your dreams. He is fully supportive of you and promises never to leave you or forsake you in your journey, and He will give you His strength where you are weak. He asks you to choose to run after purity and to trust Him, that He is protecting you and leading you into His love story for your life.

The love story that God has for you is not just a story, but your own real-life experience with Him—living in love with God. That is what we are inviting you to grab onto for yourself. That is the biggest "yes" you can ever make. You can say "yes" for other reasons, and that might get you down the purity highway for a while, but ultimately, you need God's comfort, love and grace to be able to live the life that's in your heart to live.

In order for you to one day love your spouse, you must first love yourself. The Bible is clear that we love others in the way we love ourselves *(Matthew 22:39)*. In making a purity covenant with yourself, you are promising yourself that you will love, honor and cherish the way you were made, including your sexuality. After all that we have learned about our design as human beings, it is easy to see that one of the best ways to love yourself and experience sex in its fullness, is to guard your heart and keep sex for marriage.

In saying yes to the things listed below, understand that you are inherently saying NO to other things. There is only so much room in your life, and you get to choose what will be there. Replace the bad with good, and the bad will not have room to stay. So, instead of making this a promise about the things you say NO to, it will be covenant about (a YES to) doing the right things. What you focus on, you make room for in your life; keep your eyes focused on the goal, and you'll become a winner!

In signing this covenant I, _____
am saying YES to: (PRINT NAME)

a) My value as a son or daughter of God. I will freely receive God's love, affirmation, and correction.

b) Having people in my life (eg. fathers, mothers, leaders etc) who can speak into my decisions and help me live the best life I can choose for myself.

c) Valuing my whole being by only having a sexual relationship with my spouse (future or current).

d) Staying honest and connected with my heart (emotions, thoughts and feelings) while in my process.

e) Protecting myself by being careful about what I look at, think about and touch.

f) Protecting others by my words and actions, in what I say, how I view them, how I behave towards them.

g) Being powerful and assertive in taking care of my needs in a healthy way.

h) Cultivating and celebrating my unique masculinity/femininity to honor my design as a man/woman.

i) Transparency and vulnerability. I will allow people to see me and allow myself to be known.

j) A life of integrity. I will be a person who does what I say I will do.

k) Not hiding who I am, but allowing who I am on the inside to manifest on the outside.

l) Dressing and behaving in a way that reflects who I am on the inside.

m) Respecting myself and my boyfriend/girlfriend in our mutual pursuit of each other.

n) Allowing God to meet my needs for intimacy, connection and comfort, before getting them met from a counterfeit source.

o) _____

p) _____

q) _____

While the most important YES is said first in your heart, it is important to share your choice with others. Below is a space to sign your YES. This will be a reminder to you of your brave choice and it will allow others to be a part of your process, to walk with you and celebrate every victory you have on your journey!

I, _____ **make**

this Covenant of Purity with myself and God on

_____.
      (DATE)

Witnesses: *(People who will walk with you and help you stay accountable to your YES.)*

X   _____

X   _____

X   _____

Making a Purity Plan

What's your plan? If your plan sounds something like, "My plan is to lose 10 lbs." "My plan is to not masturbate," you need to know that you do not have a plan.

What you will or will not do may be part of your plan, but it is not a plan. For example, the statement, "I will not look at pornography," is a GOAL not a PLAN. The goal is the outcome you want. The plan is the action you will take to get what you want. The statement, "I will stop lusting by asking God what He thinks about the women I find attractive," is a PLAN. Your GOAL may be included in your plan, but you need actions you will DO to get your goal.

Once you have some goals and some plans to meet your goals, share your plan with someone you are accountable to—perhaps the people who witnessed and signed your Purity Covenant—and get some feedback. Make a plan to connect with them on a set date, about once a month, if not more often. If either of you cannot commit to that, perhaps you need to find different accountability—you need to be able to have access to them, and talking with them once every three months probably won't be enough! If you have a boyfriend/girlfriend, you will want to talk about your physical relationship and boundaries and make a plan for the two of you. Share this with your accountability person/couple. This will show them what standard you've chosen for yourself and how they can help you on your journey.

Remember: you are made of a spirit, soul and body, so include something for each of those parts of you in your plan! The more specific you can be in your actions, the better. Your plan is somewhat fluid, and may change over time. This is your own personal roadmap: yours will be unique to you! Test drive your plan—if it doesn't work, or have the effect you were hoping for, change it! You may not be meeting your needs correctly, or you may have unrealistic expectations on yourself. This is a work in progress, it will change and grow as you do!

While making your plan, ask yourself these questions:

1. What are my "red-flags" and/or triggers?

   a. What are you feeling, thinking about or experiencing BEFORE you make an unhealthy choice? What was going on? This will help you identify what you were feeling, and why you were feeling it.

2. What am I feeling?

   a. Identify what you're feeling. Eg: Angry? Powerless? Inadequate? Lonely? Misunderstood? This will help highlight what you need.

3. What do I need?

   a. Identify in the moment what you need. What were you trying to get? This is important to know, so you can DO the right thing. Eg: Power? Validation? Comfort? Intimacy? Encouragement? Sleep? Is it a spirit, soul or body need?

4. What am I going to do about it?

   a. What specific action will I take to get my need met, in a healthy way (from the right source)? This is your plan. This is what you do.

My Purity Plan

SPIRIT *[Primary needs: identity, purpose, intimacy]*

EXAMPLES

1. Because of my need for confidence (identity, affirmation, etc.) I will read my Bible daily to learn what God says about me.

2. I will forgive my dad for being harsh and critical, and invite God to give me the love/affirmation I need from a Father.

3. When I make a mistake, I will not punish myself, but will repent and forgive myself. I will use that opportunity to discover more about my needs. and think about what it was that I needed at that time.

Write your own:

1.

2.

3.

4.

5.

SOUL *(Mind, Will, Emotions)*
[Primary needs: intimacy, connection, comfort]

EXAMPLES

1. When I feel depressed, low or hopeless, I will talk to God and journal about my feelings. If I need it, I will then call a friend/ family member and connect with them.

2. I will not talk on the phone/text/chat with the opposite sex after 10pm.

3. I will break the habit of looking at pornography by allowing myself to think about and feel my emotions. I will not try to distract myself when I'm hurting, but instead I will let myself cry.

Write your own:

1.

2.

3.

4.

5.

BODY *(Physical)*
[Primary Needs: Food, Water, Sleep, Human Contact]

EXAMPLES

1. I will take care of my body, including my mind and emotions, by eating healthy food and getting 8 hours of sleep every night.
2. Because I don't think straight when I'm tired, I will go to sleep instead of watching TV.
3. I will not drink alcohol when I'm out on a date, because it impairs my judgment.

Write your own:

1.

2.

3.

4.

5.

ANSWER KEY

LESSON 1

- We learn sex is not IMPORTANT
- We learn sex is just a PHYSICAL ACT
- We learn sex is both VALUABLE and SHAMEFUL
- God CREATED sex
- The purpose of sex is to be FRUITFUL & MULTIPLY!
- God's love for me is UNCONDITIONAL
- I cannot ESCAPE the presence of God
- God withholds NO GOOD THING from me

LESSON 2

- Everything was YES, but with boundaries
- It is IMPOSSIBLE for God to lie
- EVERYTHING God created is good
- God is CONSISTENT
- God sees the WHOLE picture of my life
- With God's help, there is NOTHING I can't do
- My past does not DEFINE my future
- I will HONOR you because I am HONORABLE
- I will PROTECT what has been entrusted to me
- God UNIQUELY created me with INTENTION, detail and purpose

LESSON 3

- Sex creates a connection at BODY, SOUL and SPIRIT level
- MEMORIES are built during sex
- Looking can HURT us
- Our thoughts are very POWERFUL
- Our thoughts can determine our ACTIONS

LESSON 4

- Abuse of my body needs can lead to PHYSICAL ILLNESS, OBESITY, ANOREXIA or DEATH
- These include extreme sport activities, (snowboarding, rock climbing, cliff jumping etc), laughter, exercise, food, a good movie, human interaction, connection and contact, drugs & alcohol.
- Abuse of my soul needs can lead to ADDICTION or SHUTTING DOWN my emotions.
- The key to getting our soul needs met in a healthy way is allowing our SPIRIT to be the primary source
- Abuse of my spiritual needs means something else is giving me IDENTITY
- God will FILL every need I have
- If I don't exercise self-control (allow my spirit to lead my will) I am VULNERABLE to attack
- My soul is affected by what I am FEEDING on
- When I am not living a Spirit-led life, my thoughts, emotions and desires become TOXIC and DESTRUCTIVE
- Addressing the needs of my spirit is VITAL

LESSON 5

- Premarital sex is a sin against GOD and against my BODY
- Jesus made a ONE TIME sacrifice for my sin.
- NOTHING can separate me from the love of God.
- When I go to something or someone to get my deepest needs met, I am committing ADULTERY or IDOLATRY
- God responds to my 'turning' IMMEDIATELY.
- Knowing the truth sets me FREE.
- Renewing my mind will lead to TRANSFORMATION.

- Anything the enemy tempts me with will result in DESTRUCTION
- Jesus fully EMPATHIZES with my weaknesses.
- There is NO temptation I can't overcome because God will ALWAYS provide a way out.
- A soul-tie is an EMOTIONAL BOND between two people.
- Soul-ties are healthy when they involve COVENANT and COMMITMENT.
- Sex outside of marriage creates an UNHEALTHY soul-tie.
- There is NO part of me or my life that God cannot restore.

LESSON 6

- A covenant is a BINDING PROMISE made between two people.
- God's GRACE and POWER are available to me because we are in covenant.
- My covenant with God is through CIRCUMCISION of my heart.
- Purity LOOKS like something.
- To make a plan I need to know what my RED FLAGS or TRIGGERS are.
- With God's help I can meet my needs in a HEALTHY way.
- An accountability person will take ACCOUNT for my ABILITY to do well.
- As I grow and learn I am setting myself up for SUCCESS.

ABOUT MORAL

THE FACTS

1

Cars & Contraception (60's)

In the 1950's, access to cars gave teenagers an independence unknown to the previous generation. When "the pill" came on the scene in 1960, women stopped requiring men to marry them before having sex because they no longer feared getting pregnant.

3
First US State Legalizes "No-Fault" Divorce (1970)

In 1970, Governor Ronald Reagan passed the "no-fault" divorce law in the state of California allowing marriages to be dissolved without providing proof that a breach in the marital contract had occurred. By 1985, all other states would follow. Currently, the US has an overall divorce rate of 50%. The US ranks 6th in the world for highest divorce rates.

2

First US State Legalizes Sodomy (Homosexual Acts) (1962)

In 1962, Illinois became the first state to remove criminal penalties for consensual sodomy (homosexual acts) from their criminal code. Today, about 3.8% of Americans identify as gay, lesbian, bisexual, or transgender.

4

Supreme Court Legalizes Abortion (1973)

In 1973 abortion became legal in our nation. Since the 40th anniversary of Roe vs. Wade, the US has aborted over 54 million children. In 1995, Norma McCorvey (Roe) became a Christian. She is now pro-life. In 2005, she petitioned the Supreme Court to overturn Roe vs. Wade... her petition was denied.

REVOLUTION

5 STD's and Children Born Out of Wedlock (70's – Present)

Prior to the Sexual Revolution, there were two main STDs that people were concerned about contracting. Now, there are over 25. That's more than a 1,200% increase in 50 years. Today, 1 in 4 people are infected with an STD. In 1964, only 7% of children were born out of wedlock... today, 53% of children are born in the U.S. out of wedlock.

7 Sex Slavery (Today)

There are currently over 27 million people, in 161 countries, trapped in the sex slave industry around the globe. People are sold as slaves for $90 or less. 80% of these slaves are women. 17,500 people are trafficked into the US annually. Sex slavery is a 32 billion dollar industry worldwide.

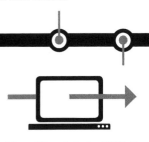

6 Internet/Porn Industry (1995 – Present)

With the launch of the internet and with the increasing popularity of smartphones, porn has now become a 5 billion dollar world-wide industry. 7 out of 10 men and 5 out of 10 women view porn regularly. Sex is the #1 topic searched on the internet.

8 THE NEW SEX RADICAL

A PERSON RADICAL ENOUGH TO QUESTION EVERYTHING AROUND THEM & GET BACK TO GOD'S ORIGINAL INTENT & DESIGN FOR GENDER, SEXUALITY, MARRIAGE, & THE FAMILY.

FOUNDER'S NOTE

Moral Revolution is an organization of radical lovers and passionate people. Like Dr. Martin Luther King, we have a dream of becoming a catalyst for a liberating global movement. We are committed to transforming how the world views sexuality, defines the unborn, embraces the family, and values all generations by honoring every human life.

We have dedicated ourselves to uncovering the root causes of moral decay that destroy the very fabric of our society. We have united under the banner of true love to help provide real solutions to these core issues and not just symptomatic cures.

It is our heart-felt conviction that a healthy culture is nurtured by positive reinforcement through intelligent and unbiased education. Honest, transparent discussion will achieve far more than fear, punishment, and rules.

WE BELIEVE THAT WHEN MOST PEOPLE ARE LOVED UNCONDITIONALLY, EQUIPPED PROPERLY, INFORMED EQUITABLY, AND EMPOWERED EQUALLY, THEY ARE PRONE TO BEHAVE NOBLY.

JOIN THE REVOLUTION, AND TOGETHER WE WILL MAKE HISTORY!

CHANGING GLOBAL MINDSETS BY CHANGING CULTURE

FAMILY

CHURCH

CULTURE

EDUCATION

GOVERNMENT

START

LITTLE ME

LEARN IT

MORAL REVOLUTION
The Naked Truth About Sexual Purity

KRIS VALLOTTON
& JASON VALLOTTON

LOVE IT

WEBSITE

PODCAST

CONFERENCES

LIVE IT

40-DAY JOURNAL

LEAD IT

REVOLUTIONIST

LEADERSHIP CURRICULUM

LEADERSHIP WORKSHOPS

STAY CONNECTED

website

facebook

twitter @MORALREVOLUTION

youtube

podcast

blog

email CONTACT@MORALREVOLUTION.COM

ADDITIONAL RESOURCES

MORAL REVOLUTION

This book takes a non-religious, gut-honest, fresh look at a subject as old as Adam and Eve. The wisdom within helps you and those you love emerge from the mire with your trophy of purity intact so you can present it to your lover on your honeymoon. While some nations seem to live in a perpetual orgy, and religion relegates the masses to sexual prison, people need to know they can overcome the power of peer pressure and push back the cesspool of distorted cultural values. You can take a Vow of Purity today—you will never regret the decision.

40-DAY JOURNALS

This Journal was created for you by people who are 100% passionate about seeing you experience health and freedom in every area of your life! Included are 40 daily topics to equip you to live with a greater understanding of how God created you, and His design for sexuality and relationships. This is a Smart-Book with embedded media throughout, furthering your interactivity and engagement beyond the written content.

REQUEST A SPEAKER

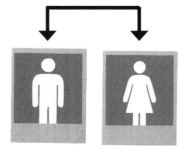

ADD AN ELEMENT

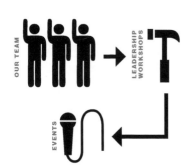

For more info, email: contact@moralrevolution.com

Join the
MORAL
REVOLUTION
AND TOGETHER
WE WILL
MAKE HISTORY

NEWSLETTER   PRAY    DONATE